Watch It Grow
Frog
Barrie Watts

W
FRANKLIN WATTS
LONDON • SYDNEY

First published in 2003 by Franklin Watts
96 Leonard Street, London EC2A 4XD

Franklin Watts Australia
45–51 Huntley Street, Alexandria, NSW 2015

© Barrie Watts 2003

Editor: Jackie Hamley
Art director: Jonathan Hair
Photographer: Barrie Watts
Illustrator: David Burroughs
Reading consultant: Beverley Mathias

A CIP catalogue record for this book
is available from the British Library

ISBN 0 7496 4762 0

Printed in Hong Kong, China

How to use this book

Watch It Grow has been specially designed to cater for a
range of reading and learning abilities. Initially children may
just follow the pictures. Ask them to describe in their own
words what they see. Other children will enjoy reading the
single sentence in large type, in conjunction with the pictures.
This single sentence is then expanded in the main text. More
adept readers will be able to follow the text and pictures by
themselves through to the conclusion of the life cycle.

Contents

Frogs come from eggs.

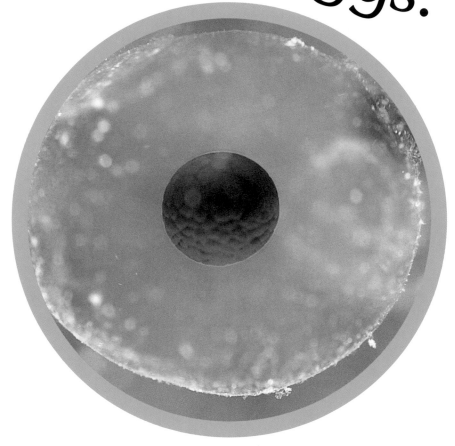

Here is an egg laid by a female frog. The egg is surrounded by a ball of jelly. Together, the egg and jelly are about the size of a pea. The jelly is tough to protect the dark egg in the middle.

A female frog lays hundreds of eggs at one time. She lays them in a pond or marsh. The eggs are all stuck together in a big lump, called **frogspawn**.

The egg changes.

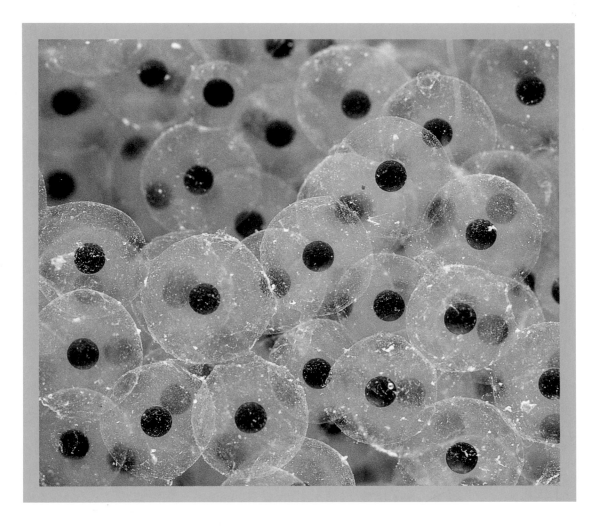

After a week the dark egg in the middle of the jelly begins to change shape. Slowly it becomes a soft, wriggling creature, about as long as a grain of rice.

A baby frog, called a **tadpole**, is growing. The **tadpole** eats food stored in the egg. After about two weeks, all the food in the egg has been used up and the jelly around it has become softer.

The tadpole hatches.

When the **tadpole** is ready to hatch, it wriggles through the soft jelly. The **tadpole** has a large head and tail. It will use its tail for swimming.

For the first few days after hatching, the **tadpole** rests. It uses a small sucker on its chin to stick to the rest of the **frogspawn** or a plant.

The tadpole breathes underwater.

In order to live, the **tadpole** needs to breathe. It has to take **oxygen** from the water. The **tadpole** breathes by using two feathery limbs, called **gills**, one on either side of its head. The **gills** take **oxygen** from the water and pass it to the **tadpole's** blood.

The **tadpole** also needs to find food. It feeds on tiny green plants called **algae**, which grow on waterweeds.

The tadpole's body changes.

After about six weeks, the
tadpole's back legs start to grow.
The **tadpole** is getting bigger.
It now eats larger foods such as
small water worms.

The feathery **gills** by its head have disappeared and the **tadpole** now breathes using **gills** inside its body. It sucks in water through its mouth, pushes it over the **gills** and out through a breathing hole, called a **spiracle**.

spiracle

The front legs grow.

Four weeks later the **tadpole** begins to grow its front legs. At first the legs look like flaps of skin. Each day they grow longer. Soon they look like a pair of legs with clawed feet on the end.

The **tadpole's** mouth and eyes are getting bigger, and its tail is slowly shrinking. The **tadpole** is beginning to look like a frog.

The tadpole uses its lungs.

When the **tadpole's** front legs grow, they close up the **spiracle**. This means that the **tadpole** cannot use the **gills** inside its body. Instead, it starts to take **oxygen** from the air.

Now the **tadpole** begins to use its **lungs**. It swims to the surface of the water to breathe in air. The **tadpole** had **lungs** when it hatched but they were too small to use at first.

The froglet comes out of the water.

After 12 weeks, the **tadpole** has turned into a **froglet** (a small frog). Its tail has become smaller, so it uses its legs to swim.

The **froglet** now spends more time out of the water. It sits on lily pads and floating weeds, or by the side of the pond, looking for small insects to eat.

The froglet can jump.

A **froglet** makes a tasty meal for **predators**. A frog's **predators** include cats and birds. If the **froglet** senses **predators** nearby, it jumps into the water for safety.

The **froglet's** strong back legs are like springs. It uses them to leap up to 10 times its body length, especially when it is young and not too heavy.

The froglet looks for food.

The **froglet** will take two years to become an adult. The **froglet** now spends most of its time on land. It hides under a rock or log during the day. At night, it comes out to look for food.

The **froglet** tries to eat any moving creature that is smaller than itself. A favourite food is worms. The **froglet** cleans the soil from the worms by pulling them through its front claws. Then it swallows them whole.

The frog sleeps through the winter.

In late autumn, frogs **hibernate**. They sleep through the winter to survive the cold. During their long sleep, they live on food they have stored in their bodies.

Female frogs and **froglets** usually hide in a damp place on land to **hibernate**. Adult male frogs usually sleep hidden in mud at the bottom of a pond. There they breathe through their skin.

The frog looks for a pond.

In early spring, the female frogs wake up and search for a pond. They always look for the pond they grew up in. They can tell this pond by the smell of the water.

Sometimes frogs travel a long way looking for the right pond, crossing roads, rivers and other ponds until they find it.

The female frog lays her eggs.

After **hibernation**, the female frog looks fat. Her body is full of the eggs that she will lay. When she arrives at the right pond, the male frogs are already waiting. The female chooses a male frog with whom to mate.

The male frog clings to her back. As she lays her eggs, he **fertilises** them. The female frog then leaves the pond and will not come back until next year. The eggs are left to hatch on their own. Soon, **tadpoles** begin to wriggle inside the **frogspawn**.

Word bank

Algae - moss-like plants that grow in water or in damp places. Tadpoles eat algae.

Fertilises - when male sperm meets a female egg, the egg is fertilised and a new life is formed. Male frogs squirt sperm onto the female's eggs to fertilise them.

Frogspawn - a lump of frog eggs stuck together.

Froglet - a young frog.

Gills - parts of the body used to take oxygen from the water. Tadpoles have two different kinds of gills.

Hibernate, Hibernation - when an animal hides away and goes into a deep sleep during the cold winter.

Lungs - bag-like organs inside an animal's body that are used to breathe air.

Oxygen - a gas found in air and water that animals need to live.

Predators - animals that hunt and eat other animals.

Spiracle - a breathing hole. A whale's blowhole is a spiracle. Tadpoles use a spiracle when they breathe through the gills inside their bodies.

Tadpole - the stage of a frog or toad before it becomes an adult.

Life cycle

A week after being laid, the frog egg starts to change into a tadpole.

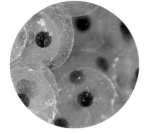

The following spring, the female frog lays her eggs.

About a week later, the tadpole hatches. It soon eats algae. It breathes using gills outside its body.

The froglet hibernates. After two years, the frog is fully grown and ready to mate.

Six weeks after hatching, the tadpole's back legs start to grow. It now breathes through its spiracle.

Twelve weeks after hatching, the tadpole has become a froglet. Its tail is smaller and its eyes are bigger.

Four weeks later, the tadpole starts to grow front legs.

As the front legs grow, the tadpole starts breathing through its lungs.

Index